CW01653041

Thai Easy Cooking

Thai Stir-fry

Thai Stir-fry

ISBN 978-616-7016-30-6
First Published July 2010 by
Sangdad Publishing Co., Ltd.
Second Printing May 2011
Price 150 Baht

Text & Photography Copyright © 2010 by
Sangdad Publishing Co., Ltd.

Managing Director Nidda Hongwiwat
Vice Managing Director Jiranan Tubniem
General Manager and Editor-in-Chief Nan Hongvivatana

Food Editor Obchoel Imsabai
Editorial Staff Oranuch Wangsuekul, Sirilak Rodyan, Yaowapa Kwandussadee, Buppha Kittikul, Kachanuj Karunrattanakul, Pattaporn Krayom
Art Director Samart Sudto **Assistant Art Director** Bhinnasak Kaewyai
Layout Ratapol Chansopa **Photography** Sangdad Studio
Proof Reader Oeung-arin Saichan, Panrawee Chai-inkam
Slides Bank Thongpoon Malasri, Aroonluk Puenpinij
Marketing Boonjarean Muansri, Chatchai Kangman
Finance Chonticha Uamduang, Wannee Tongsom, Maliwan Jenjobe
Production Napakan Khumchaiyapoom, Yuttachai Pimsalee, Kanokwan Sonsukon
Color Separation Scan Art Co., Ltd. Tel. (66) 2292-0279-81
Printer Pimdee Co., Ltd. Tel. (66) 2401-9401

Publisher and Distributor Sangdad Publishing Co., Ltd.
320 Lad Phrao 94 (Town in Town), Wangthonglang, Bangkok 10310, Thailand
Tel. (66) 2934-4414 ext. 102-110 Fax. (66) 2538-1499, (66) 2934-4415
E-mail: marketing@sangdad.com **www.sangdad.com**

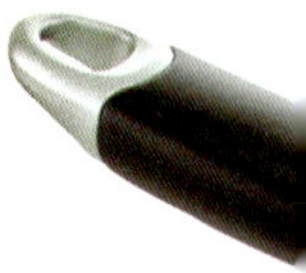

Preface

Cooking Thai stir-fried dishes is very easy. The ingredients are also very adaptable, depending on what are available in the kitchen. The rich variety of Thai stir-frying recipes offers a wide range of tasty dishes that can be enjoyed at every meal without repeating the same ones. Wonderfully created, Thai stir-frying easily becomes an exciting cooking adventure.

A basic cooking utensil is a frying pan. Any kind of pans are used: flat bottom, deep bottom, cast iron or non-stick ones.

The essential ingredient is cooking oil, which should be well selected as it is important to our health and flavor. Chicken, beef or pork stock is suggested for cooking. Vegetable stock or even water, however, remains an excellent choice. The more fresh ingredients are, the better taste the food provides.

In the Thai Stir-fry, you will explore the world of stir-frying, from the simplest recipes with a mild taste to the most vivid flavors and different levels of spiciness. The use of curry paste in stir-frying helps provide the rich sauce along with the flavorful and juicy meat that sets the Thai stir-frying apart.

This cook book also offers comprehensive tips on how to select and store the ingredients and how to cook such a flavorful stir-fried dish. Above of all, the cooking is quick and easy, which is true to the spirit of stir-frying.

Sangdad Publishing House

Contents

Introduction

Stir-frying is one of the Thai cooking techniques which is very easy and very quick. It requires very few ingredients while the cooking technique is extremely simple. One can find Thai stir-fry in myriad styles, such as stir-fried vegetables, hot and spicy stir-fried meat, or stir-fried meat in sweet and sour sauce. Stir-fried Chicken with Holy Basil is wonderful for its hot and spicy flavor from chilies and holy basil leaves. The King Prawn in Tamarind Sauce has a perfect combination of sweet, sour, and salty taste with the subtle flavor of tamarind that enhances the taste. Meanwhile, Stir-fried Beef with Oyster Sauce is flavorful from the use of oyster sauce as seasoning. Stir-fry dishes using curry pastes are also under this category.

The key to cooking delicious stir-fry dishes is the freshness and quality of the ingredients. All ingredients should be well selected and properly stored. In addition, the particular kitchen utensils - a wok and a stove - also play an important role in making a big difference to stir-fry dishes, both in appearance and flavor.

Herbs and Vegetables

Spring onion: This vegetable has a pungent smell. Select the fresh stalks without bruises or yellow ends.

Coriander: The leaves have a cool aromatic fragrance. It is preferably used for garnish. Select the medium bunch with the bright green leaves and without bruises.

Chinese celery: This stalk vegetable with a pungent smell is in the parsley family. The fresh leaves and stalks are added to enhance a unique aroma, especially to reduce the odor of meat. Select the young plants with bright green leaves.

Small garlic: This kind of Thai garlic has a strong distinctive odor. Select the bulb which has pinkish skin. Store by hanging or placing in a basket and keep in a ventilated area in order to prevent them from being rotten or spoiled.

Shallot: The essential oil in shallot has a sweet-pungent taste with spicy smell. Select the medium size with shiny violet red skin.

Ginger: It has a sharp pungent taste. The mature ginger is more aromatic and spicy than the young one.

Holy basil: Having a sharp and spicy flavor, it is usually added in many spicy stir-fry dishes like *phat cha* and *phat khee mao*. Select the fresh leaves without bruises. The small leaves provide stronger aroma than the larger ones.

Sweet basil: This herb has green leaves and light purple stems and flowers. It has subtle mint flavor and is normally used in spicy stir-fry dishes. Select the fresh and medium size.

Kaffir lime leaves: Its essential oil has a citrus aroma. Use the leaves that are not too young or too mature. Tear the leaves and immediately add to food to retain its full fragrance.

Hot chili: It has a small size but very hot so it is usually used in the hot and spicy stir-fry dishes.

Green peppercorns: Select young fruits which are still juicy as they give a tender and hot flavor. The herb can be used whole or crushed.

Seasonings

Fish sauce: This salty liquid is made by fermenting fish with salt and allows to marinate for a year or so until all flesh are completely dissolved. Select one which made from anchovies and has a crystal clear brown color, free from sediments.

Light soy sauce: A salty brown liquid, select the first grade soy sauce that is tasty and high in nutrients. Light soy sauce fermented with sugar (not molasses) is recommended.

Dark soy sauce: There are 2 types available: salt and sweet. The salty dark soy sauce is made by fermenting light soy sauce until it turns black. The sweet one is made by fermenting light soy sauce with molasses until it turns black and has a sweet salty taste.

Seasoning sauce: This non-brewed soy sauce takes short production time by using chemical process to convert the protein in the soy into amino acids. Select the soy sauce that is high in protein and contains salt less than 20%.

Oyster sauce: This thick dark brown sauce has sweet-salty taste. It is used in many stir-fry dishes.

Fermented soybean: The soy beans are fermented with wheat flour and salt until they are soft and fragrant. It is used to enhance the salty and savory flavor. Use the fermented soybean that has bright color.

Palm sugar: There are coconut and palm sugar. They are tenderly sweet with a unique aroma. Select the natural brown color without chemical additives added.

Tamarind juice: It has the sweet and acidic taste of tamarind. Select the fresh reddish brown pulp. To use, mix the tamarind pulp with small amount of warm water, sieve and pour into the container. Keep in the refrigerator.

Sriracha chili sauce: This sauce has a blend of hot, sweet, tangy, and spicy flavor. It made from hot chilies and garlic, seasoned with sugar, salt, and vinegar. The sauce is available in 3 styles: super hot, medium hot, and mild hot.

Savory Chicken with Cashew Nuts

kai phat met ma muang him ma phan

Ingredients

½	tablespoon small garlic, minced
2	tablespoons vegetable oil
300	grams chicken breast, thinly sliced
1	small onion, cut into pieces
½	cup cashew nuts, fried
¼	cup dried spur chili, cut into 1 inch long and fried
¼	cup spring onion, cut into 1 inch long
1	tablespoon fish sauce
1	teaspoon oyster sauce
1	teaspoon dark soy sauce
¼	teaspoon sugar
1	red spur chili, diagonally sliced
	fresh coriander for garnish

Preparation

1. Sauté the garlic in the oil over medium heat until it is golden and fragrant. Add the chicken and fried until just cooked. Add the onion, cashew nuts, fried chili and spring onion and toss to combine. Season with fish sauce, oyster sauce, dark soy sauce and sugar. Turn off the heat.
2. Dip out onto a serving dish. Garnish with chili slices and coriander before serving.

   (Serves 4)

Spicy Stir-fried Seafood with Holy Basil

phat ka phrao tha le

Ingredients

2	squids (200 grams each)
3	tablespoons vegetable oil
1	tablespoon garlic, minced
3	tablespoons green and red hot chilies, minced
4	mussels, boiled until shells opened, discard one side of each shell
6	prawns (50 grams each), vein, shell and heads removed but keep tails intact
¼	cup water or pork stock
1	tablespoon oyster sauce
1½	tablespoons fish sauce
½	tablespoon seasoning sauce
1-2	teaspoons sugar
½	cup holy basil leaves
	crisp-fried holy basil leaves and sliced red spur chilies for garnish

Preparation

1. Clean the squids, discard the inedible parts and split the back lengthwise. Clean again and score the inside to a crisscross pattern, cut into pieces and put aside.
2. In a pan, heat the oil over medium heat. Fry the garlic and hot chili until they are fragrant. Add mussels, squids and prawns, cooking until they are almost done. Add water or stock and season with oyster sauce, fish sauce, seasoning sauce and sugar. When everything is done, add the holy basil leaves and toss to combine. Turn off the heat.
3. Dip out onto a serving dish, garnish with crisp-fried holy basil leaves and sliced spur chilies. Serve hot.

   (Serves 2-3)

Sweet & Sour Stirred Prawns

phat priaw wan kung

Ingredients

4	cups vegetable oil
6-8	prawns (30-40 grams each), vein, shell and heads removed but keep tails intact
2	cups breadcrumbs
3	tablespoons vegetable oil
½	tablespoon garlic, minced
½	onion, cut into wedges
2	baby corns, cut
2	cucumbers, cut into pieces
½	cup pineapple, cut into pieces
1	tomato, cut into wedges
2	bell chilies, sliced
½	cup water or pork stock
3	tablespoons ketchup
3	teaspoons fish sauce
½	tablespoon vinegar
1	teaspoon sugar
3	bunches spring onion, cut into1 inch long
	fresh spring onion for garnish

Tempura batter

1	egg
1	cup cold water
1	cup tempura flour
¼	cup rice flour

Preparation

1. To prepare tempura batter: Beat the egg with water. Mix both kinds of flour with beaten egg until no lump remains. Chill in the refrigerator until the batter turns very cold.
2. In a pan, heat 4 cups of oil over medium heat. Dip the prawns in the cold batter and coat well with breadcrumbs except the tails. Deep-fry in the hot oil until they are golden and cooked through. Remove and drain on absorbent paper. Continue until finished.
3. In another pan, heat 3 tablespoons of oil over medium heat. Sauté the garlic. Add the onion when the garlic is almost golden. Cook until the onion is just done, add all vegetables and toss well. Pour in water or stock. Season with ketchup, fish sauce, vinegar and sugar. Add the fried prawns and spring onion, toss quickly and then turn off the heat.
4. Dip out onto a serving dish, garnish with spring onion and serve at once. *(Serves 2)*

Stir-fried Beef Fillet with Oyster Sauce

phat nuea nam man hoi

Ingredients

100	grams beef tenderloin, cut into bite-sized pieces
½	tablespoon light soy sauce
2	teaspoons cornstarch
2	tablespoons vegetable oil
1	tablespoon small garlic, minced
¼	onion (100 grams), cut into wedges
4	dried Shiitake mushrooms, soaked until tender and cut into wedges
¼	cup water
8	straw mushrooms, halved
2	tablespoons oyster sauce
1	tablespoon fish sauce
1	teaspoon sugar
¼	teaspoon pepper
2	bunches spring onion, cut only the white part into 1 inch long
1	red spur chili, diagonally sliced

Preparation

1. Toss the beef tenderloin with light soy sauce and cornstarch, put aside.
2. In a pan, heat the oil over medium heat. Sauté the garlic until it is almost golden. Add the onion and Shiitake mushroom, stirring lightly. Add the beef and water, cooking until the beef is done. Add the straw mushroom and toss to combine. Season with oyster sauce, fish sauce, sugar and pepper. Add the spring onion and chili, mixing well. When all ingredients are done, remove from the heat.
3. Transfer to a serving dish and serve hot.
   (Serves 2)

Fresh-Water Prawns in Sweet Tamarind Sauce

kung yai phat sauce ma kham

Ingredients

- 8 fresh-water prawns (100 grams each)
- 4 cups vegetable oil
- ¼ cup shallot, fried
- 2 tablespoons garlic, fried
- 8 dried hot chilies, fried
- fresh coriander leaves for garnish

Tamarind sauce

- 1 pickled garlic clove (20 grams), sliced
- 1 tablespoon coriander root, sliced
- 2 tablespoons vegetable oil
- ½ cup palm sugar
- 1 cup tamarind juice
- 2 tablespoons juice reserved from pickled garlic
- 3 tablespoons fish sauce

Preparation

1. To make tamarind sauce: Pound the pickled garlic and coriander root to a fine paste. In a pan, heat the oil over medium heat. Sauté the paste until it is fragrant. Add the palm sugar, cooking until it is melted. Add the tamarind juice, juice reserved from the pickled garlic and fish sauce. Reduce to low heat, simmering until the sauce is slightly thick. Remove from the heat.
2. Clean the prawns, trim off the heads and split the back lengthwise. Fry in the hot oil over high heat until they are done and remove from the pan.
3. Arrange the fried prawns nicely on a serving dish. Spoon generous amount of the tamarind sauce over. Sprinkle with fried shallot, fried garlic and chilies. Garnish with fresh coriander leaves before serving.
   (Serves 4)

Stir-fried Fish with Chinese Celery

pla phat khuen chai

Ingredients

2	cups vegetable oil
250	grams striped snake-head fish meat, cut into bite-sized pieces
1	tablespoon small garlic, minced
1	teaspoon fish sauce
2	teaspoons light soy sauce
1	teaspoon sugar
2	tablespoons water or pork stock
4	bunches Chinese celery, cut into 1 inch long
1	red spur chili, diagonally sliced
	Chinese celery sprig for garnish

Preparation

1. In a pan, heat the oil over medium heat. Fry the fish in the hot oil until it is golden crisp. Remove and drain.
2. Drain away the oil and reserve only 2 tablespoons in the same pan. Fry the garlic until it is almost golden. Add the fried fish and turn to high heat. Season with fish sauce, light soy sauce and sugar. Add the water or stock, stir-frying quickly to combine. Add the Chinese celery and spur chili, tossing. Remove from the heat.
3. Ladle onto a serving dish. Garnish with Chinese celery sprig and serve immediately.

   (Serves 2)

Spicy Stir-fried Beef with Holy Basil

phat khi mao nuea sap

Ingredients

1	teaspoon mature galangal, finely sliced
1	teaspoon black peppercorns
25	cloves small garlic
2	tablespoons hot chilies
3	tablespoons vegetable oil
250	grams beef tenderloin, coarsely minced
1½	tablespoons fish sauce
1	tablespoon light soy sauce
1	teaspoon sugar
1	kaffir lime leaf, torn
5	cloves large garlic, coarsely sliced
2	bunches green peppercorns, stalks removed
½	cup holy basil leaves
	crisp-fried holy basil leaves for garnish

Preparation

1. In a mortar, thoroughly pound the galangal and black peppercorns. Add the small garlic and hot chilies, pounding coarsely.
2. In a pan, heat the oil over medium heat. Sauté the pounded mixture until it is fragrant. Add the beef, stir-frying until cooked through. Season with fish sauce, light soy sauce and sugar. Toss to mix well. Add the remaining ingredients and then stir-fry to combine.
3. Ladle onto a serving dish. Garnish with crisp-fried holy basil leaves and then serve.

   (Serves 4)

Stirred Crab in Curry Sauce

pu phat phong ka ri

Ingredients

3	tablespoons vegetable oil
1	tablespoon curry powder
200	grams steamed crab meat
½	cup water or chicken stock
½	onion, cut into wedges
2	tablespoons fish sauce
1½	teaspoons sugar
1	teaspoon oyster sauce
1	tablespoon garlic, fried
1	red spur chili, diagonally sliced
1	bunch Chinese celery, cut into 1 inch long
1	bunch spring onion, cut into 1 inch long
	fresh Chinese celery sprig for garnish

Preparation

1. In a pan, heat the oil over medium heat. Stir in the curry powder and crab meat together. Add the water or stock and onion. Continue cooking until the onion is translucent. Season with fish suace, sugar and oyster sauce. Add the fried garlic, tossing to combine. Add spur chili, Chinese celery and spring onion. Cook until everything is done and remove from the heat.
2. Transfer to a serving dish and garnish with Chinese celery sprig. Serve hot.

   (Serves 2)

Stir-fried Vegetables and Prawns

phat phak ruam mit kap kung

Ingredients

- 4 Chinese kale tips
- 1 tablespoon garlic, minced
- 3 tablespoons vegetable oil
- 4 prawns (40 grams each), vein, shell and heads removed but keep tails intact
- 6 baby corns, halved
- 6 pods snow pea
- 6 straw mushrooms, halved
- 4 leaves Chinese cabbage, sliced
- ¼ cup water or pork stock
- 1 tablespoon oyster sauce
- 2 tablespoons light soy sauce
- ½ teaspoon sugar

Preparation

1. Place a pot of water over high heat, add small amount of salt and bring to a boil. Blanch the Chinese kale tips until they are done. Remove and soak in the cold water for a few minutes and drain.
2. Sauté the garlic in the oil until it is golden and fragrant. Add the prawns and cook until done. Add all vegetables and turn to high heat. Pour in water or stock and season with oyster sauce, light soy sauce and sugar. Toss to mix well and then remove from the heat.
3. Dip out onto a serving dish and serve hot.
   (Serves 4)

Fried Fish with Sweet & Sour Sauce

pla priaw wan

Ingredients

300	grams sea bass, sliced into ½ inch thick
2	tablespoons light soy sauce
3-4	tablespoons all-purpose flour
1	cup vegetable oil
½	onion (100 grams), cut into wedges
1	tomato (100 grams), cut into wedges
¼	cup pineapple, cut into pieces
3	tablespoons ketchup
1	teaspoon seasoning sauce
1	tablespoon vinegar
1	tablespoon sugar
½	cup water
1	tablespoon cornstarch
2	bunches spring onion, cut into 1 inch long
	coriander leaves for garnish

Preparation

1. Toss the fish with 1 tablespoon of light soy sauce and marinate for 15 minutes.
2. Toss the marinated fish with all-purpose flour and fry in the hot oil until it is almost golden on the outsides but the meat is still juicy. Remove and drain.
3. Drain away the oil and reserve only 3 tablespoons in the pan. Add the onion, tomato and pineapple. Toss and reduce to low heat. Stir in ketchup, seasoning sauce, vinegar, sugar, the remaining light soy sauce and water. Taste and adjust. Mix cornstarch with small amount of water, stirring to thicken the sauce. Add fried fish and spring onion. Toss quickly and turn off the heat.
4. Dip out onto a serving dish and garnish with coriander leaves. Serve hot. *(Serves 4)*

Stir-fried Minced Pork with Ginger

mu phat khing

Ingredients

3	tablespoons vegetable oil
1	tablespoon small garlic, minced
250	grams minced pork
¼	cup water
1	cup young ginger, julienned
1	tablespoon light soy sauce
1	tablespoon fish sauce
½	teaspoon dark soy sauce
2	teaspoons sugar
1	red spur chili, diagonally sliced
	coriander leaves for garnish

Preparation

1. In a pan, heat the oil over medium heat. Sauté the garlic until it is almost golden. Add the pork, stirring to prevent the pork from sticking together and then pour in the water. Add the ginger and cook until it is done. Season with light soy sauce, fish sauce, dark soy sauce and sugar. Add the chili and mix well. Turn off the heat.
2. Dip out onto a serving dish, garnish with coriander leaves and serve.
   (Serves 4)

Savory Mung Bean Noodles with Prawns

phat wun sen

Ingredients

- 3 tablespoons vegetable oil
- 1 tablespoon garlic, minced
- 15 prawns (20 grams each), vein, shell and heads removed but keep tails intact
- 100 grams mung bean noodles, soaked until tender and cut into short sections
- ¼ cup water or chicken stock
- 2 eggs
- ½ cup black ear mushroom, sliced
- 2 tablespoons light soy sauce
- ½ tablespoon fish sauce
- 1½ teaspoons sugar
- ¼ teaspoon pepper
- 3 green and red spur chilies, diagonally sliced
- 2 bunches spring onion, cut into 1 inch long

Preparation

1. In a pan, heat the oil over medium heat. Fry the garlic until it is golden and fragrant. Add the prawns and cook until they are almost done. Add the mung bean noodles, stir-frying to combine. Pour in the water or stock and continue cooking until the noodles are tender. Move the noodles to the side of the pan and break in the eggs. Add the black ear mushroom, stir-frying to combine. Season with light soy sauce, fish sauce, sugar and pepper. Add the chili and spring onion. Cook and toss to mix well and remove from the heat.
2. Dip out onto a serving dish and serve hot.
   (Serves 2)

Stir-fried Prawns and Snow Peas in Curry Sauce

thua lan tao phat kung phong ka ri

Ingredients

3	tablespoons vegetable oil
1	tablespoon garlic, minced
8	prawns (40 grams each), vein, shell and heads removed but keep tails intact
200	grams snow peas, stem ends removed
1	tablespoon curry powder
1½	tablespoons oyster sauce
1	tablespoon seasoning sauce
1 ½	teaspoons sugar
¼	cup water
	fried garlic for topping

Preparation

1. In a pan, heat the oil over medium heat. Fry the garlic until it is fragrant. Add the prawns and snow peas. Turn to high heat and add the curry powder. Season with oyster sauce, seasoning sauce and sugar. Pour in the water, stir-frying quickly to combine. Turn off the heat.
2. Ladle onto a serving dish and sprinkle with the fried garlic. Serve hot.
   (Serves 2-3)

Stir-fried Asparagus with Prawns

nor mai fa rang phat kung

Ingredients

10 asparagus
2 tablespoons vegetable oil
1 teaspoon small garlic, crushed
5 prawns (40 grams each), vein, shell and head removed but keep tails intact
3 tablespoons water or pork stock
1 tablespoon oyster sauce
1 tablespoon light soy sauce
1 teaspoon fish sauce
1 teaspoon sugar
fried garlic for topping

Preparation

1. Clean the asparagus and trim off the hard base. Cut into 1½-inch pieces to obtain about 200 grams of asparagus.
2. In a pan, heat the oil over medium heat. Sauté the garlic until it is almost golden. Add the prawns and cook until just done. Turn to high heat and add the asparagus. Toss to mix well and stir in the water or stock. Season with oyster sauce, light soy sauce, fish sauce and sugar. Remove from the heat.
3. Ladle onto a serving dish and top with fried garlic. Serve with cooked rice.

   (Serves 2)

Spicy Stir-fried Clams and Sweet Basil

phat hoi lai

Ingredients

1	kilogram large clams
3	tablespoons vegetable oil
1	tablespoon small garlic, crushed
8	hot chilies, crushed
1	tablespoon dark fermented soy bean
1½	tablespoons roasted chili paste
½	teaspoon sugar
1½	tablespoons oyster sauce
½	cup sweet basil leaves
1	red spur chili, diagonally sliced
	sweet basil sprig for garnish

Preparation

1. Clean the clams by soaking in a bowl of water and add 4 crushed hot chilies. Allow the clams to release all the soil. Clean again and drain.
2. In a pan, heat the oil over medium heat. Sauté the garlic until it is golden fragrant. Add the clams and turn to high heat. Add the chilies, fermented soy bean, roasted chili paste and sugar. Toss to combine. Add the oyster sauce and then cover the pan. Leave for a few minutes to let the shells open. Stir again and add sweet basil leaves and spur chili. Toss and turn off the heat.
3. Dip out onto a serving dish and garnish with sweet basil sprig before serving.

   (Serves 4)

Spicy Stir-fried Roasted Duck

pet yang phat cha

Ingredients

- 1 duck breast (250 grams)
- 30 grams small garlic, peeled
- 15 hot chilies, assorted colors
- 2 yellow spur chilies
- ½ teaspoon black peppercorns
- ¼ cup vegetable oil
- 1 tablespoon fish sauce
- 1 teaspoon seasoning sauce
- 2 teaspoons light soy sauce
- 1 teaspoon sugar
- ½ cup water
- 1 kaffir lime leaf, torn
- ½ cup wild ginger, julienned
- 2 tablespoons green peppercorns, cut into short sections
- ½ cup holy basil leaves
- 2 green and red spur chilies, diagonally sliced
- crisp-fried kaffir lime leaves for topping

Preparation

1. Clean the duck breast and pat dry. Grill over charcoal fire or roast in an oven until it is golden on the outsides and the meat turns medium rare. Slice thinly and put aside.
2. Coarsely pound garlic, both kinds of chilies and black peppercorns. Put aside.
3. Place a pan over medium heat and pour in the oil. Fry the garlic mixture until it is golden and fragrant. Add the duck breast and stir to combine. Season with fish sauce, seasoning sauce, light soy sauce and sugar. Stir in water. Add the kaffir lime leaf, wild ginger, green peppercorns, holy basil leaves and spur chili. Toss to combine and remove from the heat.
4. Ladle onto a serving dish and sprinkle crisp-fried kaffir lime leaves over the top. Serve at once.

   (Serves 2)

Stir-fried Beef Loin with Green Peppercorns

nuea phat prik thai on

Ingredients

350	grams beef tenderloin
3	yellow spur chilies, sliced
35	hot chilies, assorted colors
1	teaspoon peppercorns
25	cloves small garlic
¼	cup vegetable oil
½	cup water
¼	cup wild ginger, julienned
¼	cup green peppercorns, cut into short sections
3	kaffir lime leaves, torn
2	tablespoons fish sauce
¼	teaspoon sea salt
1	teaspoon sugar
1	tablespoon oyster sauce
2	teaspoons lime juice
1	red spur chili, diagonally sliced

Preparation

1. Clean the beef well and slice into pieces, put aside.
2. In a mortar, coarsely pound both kinds of chilies, peppercorns and garlic.
3. In a pan, heat the oil over medium heat. Sauté the pounded mixture until it is fragrant. Add the beef and cook until just done. Add the water, following with wild ginger, green peppercorns and kaffir lime leaves. Season with fish sauce, salt, sugar and oyster sauce. Toss to combine and turn off the heat. Add lime juice and red chili slices, tossing well.
4. Dip out onto a serving dish and serve.
   (Serves 4)

Spicy Stir-fried Seafood Mixed

tha le phat ruea po

Ingredients

1	teaspoon peppercorns
1	tablespoon coriander root, sliced
3	tablespoons small garlic
7	hot chilies
¼	teaspoon sea salt
3	tablespoons vegetable oil
150	grams grouper meat
150	grams squid, cut into pieces
1	tablespoon fish sauce
1	teaspoon sugar
¼	cup water or pork stock
	fresh coriander leaves and crushed hot chilies for garnish

Preparation

1. In a mortar, coarsely pound peppercorns, coriander root, garlic, hot chilies and salt. Put aside.
2. In a pan, heat the oil over medium heat. Sauté the chili mixture until it is fragrant. Add fish meat and squid, tossing to combine. Season with fish sauce and sugar. Add water or stock and combine well. Cover and continue cooking for a few minutes until everything is done. Remove the cover and turn off the heat.
3. Transfer to a serving dish. Garnish with fresh coriander leaves and crushed hot chilies. Served hot with cooked rice or boiled rice.
(Serves 2-3)

Spicy Stir-fried Fish

phat phet pla

Ingredients

- 3 tablespoons vegetable oil
- 1 tablespoon garlic, minced
- 2 tablespoons red hot chilies, chopped
- 350 grams striped snake-head fish meat, sliced into bite-sized pieces
- ¼ cup water or pork stock
- ½ teaspoon black pepper
- 1 tablespoon oyster sauce
- 1 teaspoon seasoning sauce
- 1½ tablespoons fish sauce
- 1 teaspoon sugar
- ½ cup holy basil leaves
- 1 red spur chili, diagonally sliced
- crisp-fried holy basil leaves for garnish

Preparation

1. In a pan, heat the oil over medium heat. Sauté the garlic and hot chili. Cook until it is fragrant. Add the fish meat. Stir-fry lightly and continue cooking until just done. Add the water or stock and turn to high heat. Add the seasonings, tossing. Add the holy basil leaves and spur chili, tossing again. Turn off the heat.
2. Ladle onto a serving dish and garnish with crisp-fried holy basil leaves. Best when served with cooked rice.
   (Serves 4-5)

Fried Sea Bass with Crunchy Herbs

phat pla bai ma krut krop

Ingredients

1	sea bass (about 600 grams)
1	cup vegetable oil
2	tablespoons tapioca flour
¼	cup green hot chilies
2	green spur chilies, diagonally sliced
¼	cup green peppercorns, cut into short sections
¼	cup kaffir lime leaves, torn
1	tablespoon black peppercorns, lightly crushed
1	tablespoon + 2 teaspoons fish sauce
1	tablespoon seasoning sauce
1½	teaspoons sugar
	red hot chilies and fresh coriander leaves for garnish

Preparation

1. Scale the fish and remove the gills and gut. Clean well. Fillet both sides of the fish. Slice each fillet into bite-sized pieces and reserve the bone.
2. In a pan, heat the oil over medium heat. Toss the fish with tapioca flour and deep-fry until it is golden and cooked through. Remove and drain. Fry the fish bone until it is golden and crisp. Remove and drain.
3. In a bowl, combine both kinds of chilies, green peppercorns, kaffir lime leaves and black peppercorns together. Put aside.
4. Drain away the oil in the frying pan and reserve only ¼ cup in the pan. Add the chilies, peppercorns and kaffir lime leaves. Turn to high heat up. Toss and cook until kaffir lime leaves become glossy and crispy. Add the fried fish and all seasonings. Toss quickly and turn off the heat.
5. Place the fried fish bone on a serving plate and arrange the savory fried fish and herbs on top. Garnish with red hot chilies and coriander leaves before serving.

   (Serves 4)

Soft-Shelled Crabs with Black Pepper Sauce

pu nim phat phrik thai dam

Ingredients

2 soft-shelled crabs (125 grams each)
1 cup tempura flour
2 cups vegetable oil
2 tablespoons large garlic, lightly crushed
1 tablespoon red spur chilies, roughly chopped
1 onion (100 grams), diagonally sliced
4 red and green spur chilies, diagonally sliced
2 teaspoons black peppercorns, coarsely pounded
1 tablespoon fish sauce
1 tablespoon seasoning sauce
1 teaspoon sugar
4 bunches spring onions, cut into 1 inch long
fresh coriander for garnish

Preparation

1. Thaw the crabs and clean thoroughly. Quarter each crab and toss with the tempura flour while they are still wet so that they are well coated. Deep-fry in the hot oil over medium heat until cooked through and crispy. Remove and drain off the excess oil.
2. Preheat another pan over medium heat. Add 3 tablespoons of oil reserved from the fried crabs. Sauté the garlic and chopped chili until they are fragrant. Add the onion and sliced chili, tossing well. Add the fried soft-shelled crabs and the remaining ingredients. Turn to high heat and toss quickly to combine well. Turn off the heat.
3. Ladle onto a serving dish, garnish with fresh coriander and serve immediately.

(Serves 4)

Sweet and Sour Pork Ribs

si krong mu phat priaw wan

Ingredients

- 1 kilogram pork ribs, cut into 2-inch pieces
- 2 tablespoons cornstarch
- 1 teaspoon pepper
- 1 teaspoon sea salt
- 1 teaspoon Chinese wine
- 1 tablespoon light soy sauce
- 4 cups vegetable oil
- ¼ cup red spur chilies, diagonally sliced
- ½ cup pineapple, diced
- ¼ cup tomato, cut into wedges
- ½ cup onion, slice into rings
- coriander sprig for garnish

Sweet and sour sauce

- ½ cup ketchup
- 1 tablespoon young ginger, julienned
- ½ teaspoon pepper
- 1¼ teaspoons sea salt
- 2 tablespoons sugar
- 1 tablespoon vinegar
- 2 cups water or pork stock

Preparation

1. In a mixing bowl, toss the ribs with 1 tablespoon of cornstarch, pepper, salt, Chinese wine and light soy sauce. Allow to marinate for 2-3 hours. Fry the marinated ribs in the hot oil over medium heat until they are golden and cooked through. Remove and drain. Arrange nicely on a serving dish and put aside.
2. To make sweet and sour sauce: Combine everything in a saucepan and bring to a boil over medium heat. Reduce to low heat and continue simmering for 15 minutes. Turn off the heat.
3. Add ¼ cup of oil in a pan and place over medium heat. When the oil is hot, fry spur chili, pineapple, tomato and onion. Add sweet and sour sauce and cook to combine. Mix the remaining cornstarch with 3 tablespoons of water and stir into the pan. Cook and stir continuously until the sauce is clear and thick. Remove from the heat. Spoon the sauce over fried ribs, garnish with coriander sprigs and serve immediately.
   (Serves 6)

Savory Chili Chicken

kai phat phrik haeng

Ingredients

250	grams chicken breast, cubed
1	tablespoon tapioca flour
2	tablespoons light soy sauce
3	tablespoons vegetable oil
1	mature ginger, peeled and lightly crushed
1	teaspoon sugar
5	dried spur chilies, cut into 1 cm long and fried
	fresh Chinese kale

Preparation

1. Toss the chicken breast with tapioca flour and 1 tablespoon of light soy sauce. Allow to marinate in a refrigerator for 30 minutes.
2. In a pan, heat the oil over medium heat. Sauté the ginger until it is fragrant. Add the marinated chicken and cook until done. Season with the remaining light soy sauce and sugar. Continue cooking until the chicken becomes golden brown, add the fried chili and toss to combine. Remove from the heat.
3. Dip out onto a serving dish. Enjoy while hot with fresh Chinese kale.
   (Serves 2)

Stir-fried Squid with Salted Egg Yolk

muek phat khai khem

Ingredients

3	boiled salted egg yolks, cut into small pieces
¼	cup + 2 tablespoons vegetable oil
1	tablespoon small garlic, minced
300	grams squid, cut into pieces
¼	cup water
1	tablespoon oil reserved from roasted chili paste
1	tablespoon fish sauce
2	teaspoons sugar
2	teaspoons light soy sauce
3	bunches spring onion, cut into 1 inch long
1	red spur chili, diagonally sliced
	coriander leaves for garnish

Preparation

1. Blend the egg yolks with ¼ cup + 1 tablespoon of oil to a fine mixture, put aside.
2. In a pan, heat the remaining oil over low heat. When the oil is hot, stir in the egg yolk mixture. Add the garlic and fry until it turns golden. Add the squid and turn to high heat. When it is done, pour in the water and roasted chili paste oil. Season with fish sauce, sugar and light soy sauce. Add the spring onion and spur chili, tossing quickly to combine. Turn off the heat.
3. Dip out onto a serving dish, garnish with coriander leaves and serve. *(Serves 4)*

Spicy Stir-fried Chicken with Bamboo Shoot

phat phet kai nor mai

Ingredients

3	tablespoons vegetable oil
3	tablespoons instant red curry paste
170	grams chicken breast, skinned and sliced into bite-sized pieces
½	cup water
150	grams young bamboo shoot, thinly sliced and blanched
2	tablespoons fish sauce
2	teaspoons sugar
2	tablespoons evaporated milk
½	cup sweet basil leaves
2	spur chilies, diagonally sliced

Preparation

1. In a pan, heat the oil over medium heat. Sauté the curry paste until it is fragrant. Add the chicken and cook until done. Stir in the water. Add the bamboo shoot and stir-fry to combine. Season with fish sauce and sugar. Add the evaporated milk, sweet basil leaves and spur chili. Toss again and then turn off the heat.
2. Dip out onto a serving dish and serve hot with cooked rice.
   (Serves 2-3)

Stir-fried Prawns with Hot Chilies

kung phat prik khi nu

Ingredients

1½	cups vegetable oil
12	prawns (40 grams each), vein, shell and heads removed but keep tails intact
1	tablespoon + 1 teaspoon fish sauce
1½	teaspoons sugar
1	tablespoon black peppercorns, lightly crushed
3	tablespoons green peppercorns, cut into short sections
6	kaffir lime leaves, torn
¼	cup green hot chilies

Preparation

1. In a pan, heat the oil over medium heat. When the oil is very hot, fry the prawns until they are crisp and cooked through. Remove and put aside. Drain away the oil and reserve 3 tablespoons in the pan. Return the fried prawns to the pan and season with fish sauce and sugar. Turn to high heat. Add the black peppercorns, green peppercorns, kaffir lime leaves and hot chilies, mixing well. Stir-fry until kaffir lime leaves and green peppercorns turn shiny green. Remove from the heat.
2. Dip out onto a serving dish and serve.
   (Serves 4)

Stir-fried Ear Mushroom with Minced Pork and Egg

het hu nu phat khai

Ingredients

2	tablespoons vegetable oil
½	tablespoon garlic, minced
100	grams minced pork
200	grams black ear mushroom, sliced
2	eggs
1½	tablespoons light soy sauce
1½	tablespoons oyster sauce
1½	teaspoons sugar
1	teaspoon pepper
2	tablespoons spring onion and coriander leaves, sliced
	diagonally sliced red spur chilies for garnish

Preparation

1. In a pan, heat the oil over medium heat. Sauté the garlic until it is golden and fragrant. Add the pork and cook until done. Put in ear mushroom, tossing and adding small amount of water. Break in the eggs and turn to high heat. Stir-fry until the eggs are almost cooked. Season with light soy sauce, oyster sauce, sugar and pepper. Continue cooking until everything is combined and slightly dried. Add the spring onion and coriander leaves, mixing well. Remove from the heat.
2. Ladle onto a serving dish. Garnish with sliced red spur chilies and serve with cooked rice or boiled rice.
   (Serves 4)

Thai Easy Cooking

www.sangdad.com